PRAISE FOR
THE FUTURE BOOK

"Magnus Lindkvist is the grand wizard of trendspotting and future-thinking. The Future Book will enable you to see the world through his brain."

Dr Kjell A Nordström, Global Top 15 Management Guru and author of *Funky Business: Talent Makes Capital Dance*

"There are two modes of exploring the future: awaiting it or shaping it. The former is about asking knowledgeable people what they think might happen and then dreaming up what connections that might imply for you. Usually fun, very safe and in reality quite pointless. The latter – shaping – is about deep awareness there is no future other than the one you create, making best use of favourable circumstances around you. Often unsettling, sometimes unsafe and far more rewarding. Thought leader Magnus Lindkvist sits firmly in this second camp. Achievers of the future, as he calls them. Rightly so – how many visionary leaders relied on trend reports to make their future a success? None.

His latest book will not offer the easy answers you might hope for from the world's leading futurologist. It's better than that: he shows how to think about it. Lindkvist channels his expertise with a very personal focus and starts from the inside out. What does it take to shape your future, to expand your horizon and not miss or ignore the opportunities right in front of you? Then he moves on to revealing how to apply that mind-set and insight into something productive, owning that future as your own.

Lindkvist's book will arm you with the framework to navigate an endlessly complicated, beautiful future ahead; and participate. Not merely sit by the side-lines as a spectator, in awe of the smart things others are doing and wondering if it matters to you."

Costas Papaikonomou, frounder of Happen and author
of Thoughts from A Grumpy Innovator

FOR
MIRA AND MUSTAFA

THE
FUTURE
BOOK

40 WAYS TO FUTURE-PROOF
YOUR WORK AND LIFE

MAGNUS LINDKVIST

LONDON
MADRID
MEXICO CITY

NEW YORK
BARCELONA
MONTERREY
SHANGHAI

BOGOTA
BUENOS AIRES
SAN FRANCISCO

Published by
LID Publishing Ltd
One Adam Street
London
WC2N 6LE
United Kingdom

31 West 34th Street, Suite 8004,
New York, NY 1001, US

info@lidpublishing.com
www.lidpublishing.com

A member of:

BPR
Business Publishers Roundtable

www.businesspublishersroundtable.com

Printed in Spain

ISBN: 978-1-910649-24-4

Cover and page design: Laura Hawkins

CONTENTS

INTRODUCTION: WHERE IS THE FUTURE?

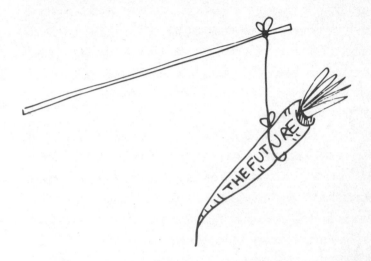

Just ahead of you lies a magical place where anything can happen. Ahead of you in time that is. Modern civilization and adulthood has taken away our beliefs in Atlantis, heaven and Santa Claus but we still believe that somewhere, on the other side of the horizon, we will find flying cars, Mars colonies, eternal life or enough wealth and prosperity to share among us. If we take the right turn. Otherwise, general doom and misery awaits and no warning is strong enough about the future dystopia. The future is not so much a precise destination in time as a kind of mind game of "what ifs". Optimists battle pessimists for attention and resources. Our hedonistic side insists on another glass of wine or slice of key lime pie while our better inner halves argue in favour of abstaining. The future arrives with an answer but has by then been transformed into the far less magical present and soon into the oblivion of the past. It's what lies ahead that we still have a chance to alter. It's what lies ahead that we can still fantasize about. It's what lies ahead that attracts, repels, titillates and stimulates us. This book is a short guide to how we could mould the future, give it a different shape, channel our expectations and maybe – just maybe – make a decision that we will not regret, maybe even celebrate at that magical moment when "then" becomes "now". Let the journey to tomorrow begin!

The future, simply put, begins in a few minutes' time. Why not immediately? Because we don't need any imaginative capability to predict what direction a tennis ball will travel when dropped from a second storey window. Harvard psychology professor Daniel Gilbert calls this "nexting" and almost all living species can do it, which is why flies dodge swatting hands and dogs fall for the same "throwing a fake ball" trick every time. If we fast forward a few minutes, however, the relationships are no longer causal and linear. In fact, a few minutes from now, the world will slowly become invisible. This is why tomorrow is a bit more uncertain than right now and why the world in 30 years' time is a lot more uncertain than the world next year. We simply don't know what it will be like. We can guess, extrapolate, wonder and fantasize but the future remains a mystery. This is why it is such an attractive and scary place on the timeline. What is unseen triggers our imagination, something that is successfully exploited by horror filmmakers, lingerie marketeers and science fiction writers alike. Future thinking, in other words, is not an exercise in logical thinking. We talk a lot about "big data" today but data is information about the past or present, not the future. We cannot model that which has not yet happened. Modelling the future on data from the past or present is merely one of many ways in which we can guess or fantasize. In other words, we should not resign ourselves to the lazy viewpoint that future thinking is better handled by others – Nobel prize-winning professors or expensive supercomputers. We have the imaginative capacity to start filling this invisible void with content, images and ideas but we may need to dust off and sharpen our brain tools to feel somewhat confident in our role as armchair futurologists.*

* A futurologist is someone who thinks about the future *and* about how we (should) think about it as opposed to a futurist who focuses mainly on what they think will happen in the future.

BOOK OVERVIEW:
THE TOOLBOX

You may only want to spend a few minutes in the company of this book so let me shoot a bullet through it – ie race through the most essential future-thinking tools and models. They will be covered in greater depth later, and even though I really think you should take the time to read it all, your busy-ness is none of my business so here is a one-minute overview.

PART ONE:
BE A POSSIBILIST

Most of us spend the little time we spend on planning for the future worrying that something bad will happen. Whether it's climate change wreaking havoc or the economy tanking so that we all lose our jobs, pessimism is a favourite pastime. Only on rare occasions do we have the audacity to be optimistic but this is mainly regarding short-term gains like job promotions or getting lucky (in all senses of the phrase). Our propensity for pessimism has evolutionary roots. Those who worried more tended to survive because the genes for worrying survived whereas the genes for saying "ho-hum, nothing to worry about" often led to the deaths of their carriers. We are not slaves to our biological heritage but worrying is still socially encouraged today. The rampant optimist is often viewed as a kind of utopian fool whereas the pessimist is viewed as a genius. This is why you should always say things like "I can see some problems ahead" or "there are clouds on the horizon" and avoid things like "that's a brilliant idea! There are no downsides!"

There is a third way to think ahead, however, and that is to stay away from narratives altogether. When we veer towards optimism or pessimism, we inadvertently tell a moral fable about tomorrow where the outcomes are understood to be – using today's evaluation metrics – good or bad. That is a leap of faith bordering on the fantastic. There are so many things ahead of us that we couldn't possibly fathom let alone place in the good or bad pile. We should, in other words, be "possibilists". The possibilist never uses the words "good" or "bad" but agnostically distinguishes between certain and uncertain futures. What can we know and what can we never know?

 **PART TWO:**
USE THE CONE OF UNCERTAINTY
WHEN LOOKING AHEAD

Actually, it's more of a funnel-shaped telescope through which you peer at tomorrow's world. In the short-run, things are not particularly incredible (hence the narrow part of the funnel) but the further ahead you look – the widening of the telescope – the more open minded you have to be about possibilities and impossibilities.

PART THREE:
THINK IN PACE LAYERS

The bestselling travel guide *1,000 Places to See Before You Die* gives a bit of a stretch goal to us humans who usually die before we turn 100. It is impossible to follow the advice, however, if you're a dragonfly. The reason we have time is so that everything doesn't happen at once, as Einstein quipped, and time, in turn, moves at different paces. Some things, like fashion, change on a whim whereas others – evolution comes to mind – are so slow as to become invisible to the human eye. This is pace-layered thinking and divides changes along different velocities to help us manage our expectations about what can happen in life and society, and when.

PART FOUR:
DISTINGUISH BETWEEN HORIZONTAL AND VERTICAL CHANGE

The future has already happened. Parts of it anyway. If you live in a modern city such as London, New York or Singapore it will be full of technologies, gadgets and lifestyle attributes that might, some day, make it to some less fortunate countries around the world. This is why we describe some places as "emerged" and others as "emerging". From another perspective, however, the future arrives unexpectedly from some unknown direction – a laboratory, the garage of some startup or the head of an artist. This is why we distinguish between horizontal changes – the same things happening in more places – and vertical changes wherein something previously impossible, even magical, becomes a reality.

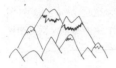

PART FIVE:
A LANDSCAPE OF MOUNTAINS, NOT STRAIGHT LINES

We have a tendency to see our life and business through a one-dimensional curve, whether it's our ageing years or fortune accumulation or our business results improving over time. In reality, we live in a world of mountains where we climb up one mountain only to reach the summit one day and be forced to climb down it and up another one if we are to find greater happiness, prosperity or profits.

PART SIX:
CREATING THE FUTURE

The future is something to be achieved, not predicted. How can we, as human beings, hunt for the clues to constructing something new, different, maybe better for our children and ourselves? It all starts by looking for secrets hiding in our midst, then experimenting to find what works and finally recycling the failures when they happen. If you are tempted to read only one of the sections of The Future Book, read this one.

PART SEVEN:
BEWARE THE PITFALLS
OF FUTURE THINKING!

Finally, this wouldn't be a proper future thinking manual if it didn't contain some advice on do's and don'ts. Here is a bite-size summary of the most common mistakes we make when thinking about the future:

■ Assuming bad things will improve and good things remain the same in the future
■ Believing that our possibilities narrow with time
■ Forgetting the future's eternal companion: the unexpected

Finally, to wrap up and summarize this short book, there will be a list of all the takeaways from each section so if you don't want to dwell on things, jump to the conclusion right now. The rest of us will now move on and look at the ideas in more depth, in the hope that they will help us become masterful futurologists.

PART ONE

BE A
POSSIBILIST

SECTION ONE:
THE PRISON
OF THE PRESENT

In the short term, nothing is possible and every new idea is seen as somewhat stupid and possibly dangerous. This is why inventors and pioneers have historically had to withstand all kinds of abuse. We are condemned to live in a prison of the present where the walls are made of myths about how fantastic our modern world is and how dangerous it would be to venture beyond it. It's very difficult to escape this prison. Most of what we think and feel is connected to the here and now. Most of us choose a life of convenience where we are fairly popular, fit into society's norms and enjoy the company of friends every now and then.

Nevertheless, if we want to live in a future that is different to today, somebody – perhaps you – needs to start looking for ways to escape this imprisonment. You will know you have succeeded when people start shouting abuse and call for the banning of whatever you propose. This is true whether we are talking about biologists studying the potential of genetic programming, activists calling for equal rights regarding minorities or someone who has found a completely new way of creating art. The future is nothing if not deviating from today's norm and its proponents are labelled deviants.

TAKEAWAY: GO ON, BE A DEVIANT!

SECTION TWO:
NARRATIVE TRAPS

We are pattern-seeking, storytelling animals. This is why our history books often read like works of fiction wherein protagonists bravely fight off the bad guys and thereby create a better world for us all. We want to simplify the complexities of life into a "right versus wrong" narrative, see resolutions in the plot and use logical causalities that make sense. This is why we fall into a narrative trap when we think about the future. Imagine you are the finance minister of Finland in the late 1980s and are asked to predict what the coming decades will bring for the Finnish economy. You would no doubt answer that Finland would prosper from the Glasnost of the Soviet Union in the east and the integration of the European Community in the west. This would create a greater demand for forestry, paper manufacturing and mining, all flourishing industries in Finland at the time. Fast forward 20 years and what actually happened was that Finland indeed prospered in its core industries – even though the Soviet Union collapsed – but more importantly, the country became a world leader in producing elevators, mobile phones and games with names such as *Angry Birds* and *Clash of Clans*. Good news for the Finnish economy but bad news for financial ministers tasked with trying to figure out where the economy was heading. The same would have been true for defence ministers who would have spent the majority of the 20th century competing in arms races with other countries, only to be attacked by 19 hijackers armed with basic utility knives.

The narrative trap happens because we respect the rules of a good story. You cannot introduce foreign elements or new characters into the middle of a story unless you want to be accused of employing *deus ex machina*. So when ministers ponder what lies beyond the horizon, they prefer to tell an engaging, coherent story that makes sense rather than predict some kind of nihilistic, plotless spectacle. This is why religion works so well as a governing tool in people's life – it adds meaning. Your life is a quest, not just a genetic accident. The accidental meeting is interpreted as a sign from above. Being fired from that job as a trigger to change direction. These psychological constructs are fine as coping mechanisms but can also blind us. This is why people use words like "unfair" or "not her of all people" when someone who has never smoked a single cigarette is diagnosed with cancer. Or why people stay in abusive relationships or dead-end jobs, preferring the false security of the known path to the many *deus ex machina* mysteries luring outside.

TAKEAWAY: DON'T SEE YOUR LIFE AS A STORY – SEE IT AS A PLOTLESS SPECTACLE!

SECTION THREE:
PESSIMIST OR OPTIMIST?

Here's a five-second guide to being a genius: Walk into any meeting without preparing, look as if you are listening intently and then pronounce, with a deep sigh: "I can see some problems with this." It doesn't matter what was being discussed, people will assume that you have been blessed with the gift of prophecy and that you are thinking several steps ahead. The guide on how to come across as a fool is equally concise: Just say "what a brilliant idea!" to whatever is proposed. People will assume you are one of those happy-go-lucky simpletons whose very presence jeopardizes everything.

Favouring pessimism is hard-wired into us for the simple reason that the genes for worrying had a greater chance of survival, as they made carriers more cautious. Fortunately, most of us don't risk being killed, eaten or slain on a daily basis anymore but the genetic programme labelled "worry!" is still encoded in us. This is why pessimistic chief economists are viewed as wise and utopian entrepreneurs considered naïve. Above all, each side will view the other with disdain and simply describe themselves as realists while pointing to supporting historical examples.

Alas, neither side is right. Both are shades of the narrative trap described in the previous section. Pessimism and optimism are lenses through which we transform reality into a kind of moral fable. Furthermore, the lenses blind us from expanding our horizons beyond good and bad. We used to think the future would bring us flying cars; instead it brought us Gangnam Style, which nobody predicted. It is the world's most viewed movie clip ever and made its creator a multi-millionaire. We see this kind of phenomena everywhere. In the 1950s, the World Health Organization predicted that polio would be the biggest challenge humanity would face in 20th century; yet within a decade, it was eradicated. What we need is "possibilism" – an ability to think beyond the present and be open minded for Gangnam Style elements – fantastic and unpredictable as they may be – before they happen. In the words of acclaimed science fiction author Arthur C Clarke: "When a distinguished but elderly scientist states that something is possible, he is almost certainly right. When he states that something is impossible, he is very probably wrong."

TAKEAWAY: BE A PESSIMIST IF YOU WANT TO SEEM SMART, AN OPTIMIST IF YOU WANT TO SEEM STUPID OR A POSSIBILIST IF YOU WANT TO BE RIGHT...IN THE LONG RUN.

SECTION FOUR:
BE A CONTRARIAN!

Here's a tip on how to predict the future accurately: Contradict everyone all the time. Unfortunately, it's also a tip for how to lose friends and alienate people. Conventional wisdom is conventional for a reason – it's socially safe. Before the printing press was invented, if we didn't like an idea, we would simply kill the person with the controversial idea and live on in blissful ignorance. Every civilization has its own truths and to challenge them is to play with fire. In fact, the idiom "to play with fire" probably comes from a time when we were living in constant darkness only to have somebody invent fire and burn himself/herself or others while doing so.

Yet if nobody plays with fire, we will never get anywhere. Alfred Nobel, the inventor of dynamite, started by randomly blowing things up, including his younger brother. You don't have to blow up your siblings but neither should you seek agreement on everything all the time. If we all agree on something that will be proved wrong in the future, we are all wrong. The person who speaks out and challenges the "truth" becomes inconvenient, anti-social and wrong... even though he or she is the only one who will be right in the future. This is why you should seek the strength to challenge others – especially those who are viewed as experts, as we shall see in the next section.

TAKEAWAY: SAVOUR THE MOMENT WHEN OTHERS CALL YOU AN IDIOT – IT MIGHT MEAN YOU ARE ON THE RIGHT PATH.

SECTION FIVE:
IGNORE THE PREDICTIONS OF THOSE WHO ARE NEITHER STUPENDOUSLY WEALTHY NOR DIRT-POOR!

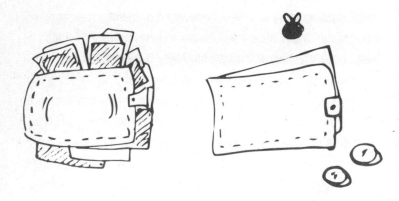

Political scientist Philip Tetlock conducted a famous experiment wherein he asked experts of all kinds to predict the future, particularly within the realm of geo-political development. Not only were they asked to make a prediction, they were also asked how certain they were of their own prediction. When he revisited the answers years later it turned out that nearly everyone had been wrong and, curiously, those who had been very certain of their own predictions were even more off the mark than those who had been somewhat ambivalent. Two conclusions are commonly made from Tetlock's study: First, the future cannot be predicted and second, we should be cautious of taking advice from self-confident know-it-alls who speak with great certainty about what lies ahead.

The first conclusion is a moot point given that the unpredictable nature of the future is what gives it its lustre. The second conclusion is probably right but very boring. Imagine if Dustin Hoffman had received the following career advice in the film *The Graduate*: "Well, I think you should try to look into the world of mainframe computing and miniaturization, there might be something interesting happening there...but I don't know, it's your life really." Even though the advice would have been accurate in hindsight, Hoffman's character would have forgotten this almost instantly, as would the movie audience. Instead, he got the iconic movie quote: "One word: plastics!" Regardless of how accurate the career advice is, it makes Hoffman think and helps him decide what kind of life he wants to avoid. The role of predictions is not necessarily to be right but to shake things up – a kind of intellectual acupuncture.

TAKEAWAY: WHEN WE SEEK ADVICE, WE SEEK CONFIDENCE IN OTHERS. THAT'S WHY THE RULE OF THUMB FOR OTHER PEOPLE'S PREDICTIONS SHOULD BE AS FOLLOWS: IGNORE THE PREDICTIONS OF THOSE WHO DON'T MOVE YOUR MIND IN AN INTERESTING, UNEXPECTED DIRECTION AND OF THOSE WHO HAVEN'T HAD THE CONFIDENCE TO PUT A LOT AT STAKE IN THEIR DECISIONS.

SECTION SIX:
EXPAND THE HORIZON

So far, we have looked at the future as a kind of societal battleground where opportunities and ideas fight for attention and resources. There is another, perhaps more important, frontier for future-thinking and that is our own lives. We are the only creatures that have the capability to think abstractly about the world and adjust our decisions and behaviour accordingly. It's a mental tool that we should cherish and learn to use even more, yet self-help books and magazines constantly advise us to live in the moment, be mindful and fully present here and now. The assumption is that too much thinking is somehow bad for your brain.

In reality, studies have shown that people who think about the future a lot tend to be more optimistic, make better choices regarding food and fitness as well as being better off financially. True, obsessing about things over which we have no control ("what's going to happen to my children in the future?") is bound to cause stress, but Ignoring the future is equally perilous ("100 cinnamon buns...just for me...yum!"). Being clinically depressed is signified by a loss of faith in the future, which is why those with depression fail to realize that things will be different tomorrow and no amount of telling them that "things will get better" will help. We don't even have to go as far as clinical depression to understand the impact of future thinking. Many of us have found ourselves stuck in relationships and dead-end jobs and grown increasingly despondent because we cannot see a way out. The future – previously majestic and infinite – has been shrunk to a binary choice of being stuck between a rock and a hard place. This is why we should always seek to expand the horizon, especially in our own lives. Just as we buy insurance because unknown bad things could happen to us in the future, we should consider *exsurance* too, which is a way of saying to yourself that unknown good things could happen.

TAKEAWAY: WHEN STUCK IN THE MIDST OF A DILEMMA, ALWAYS ADD A THIRD CHOICE EVEN, ESPECIALLY, IF IT SCARES YOU.

SECTION SEVEN:
THE SILENT FUTURE

Renowned management guru Peter Drucker once said that the biggest challenge managers face is that they mistake what is urgent for what is important. Anyone with an unbalanced worklife – everyone with a job and a life, in other words – will know the feeling of constantly having to react to outside stimuli, be it Bob coming over to chat, an email pinging into your in-box, a phone call, and so on in an endless cacophony.

Being busy is not just a nuisance; it's a way of feeling alive and seeming like you matter. Unfortunately, it is also a great way of missing out on the future. Busy-ness is actually a kind of laziness in that most of the things we do on a daily basis don't matter and reacting to stimuli can be a perfect substitute for thinking. The future is a quiet place, it has few means of competing for your attention in all the pinging, ringing, haha'ing and ker-shing'ing surrounding you on a daily basis. Yet it's waiting out there for you. Don't close yourself off to the weak signals in the world and in your life. The remedy for busy-ness is as deceptively simple as it is impossible to master: schedule time for nothing. Make it a weekly ritual where you do absolutely nothing and only listen to the sounds of the silent future. You may stumble on unknown opportunities, discover secrets, reconnect with a lost part of your personality or just discover something that makes you smile...or frown.

TAKEAWAY: THE FUTURE HIDES IN NOTHINGNESS.

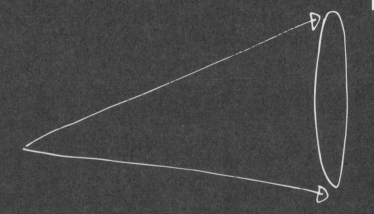

PART TWO

THE CONE OF
UNCERTAINTY

SECTION ONE:
SDRAWKCAB

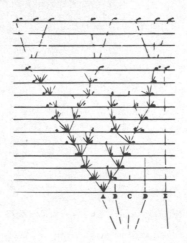

The notoriously gloomy philosopher Soren Kierkegaard said it well: "Life can only be understood backwards, but it must be lived forwards." Military strategists are on to something similar when they warn against the perils of fighting the past war instead of the current one. Risks are calculated on the past. Knowledge is dead information. What we believe we know today is based on information from the past and can be proven disastrously wrong tomorrow. Yet, in the words of less gloomy philosopher Karl Popper: "What we know next will change what happens next and we can't know what we'll know next since if we could we'd know it now." Or to put it more clearly, in the words of a man who is neither gloomy nor a philosopher, economist John Kay: "You can never predict something like the invention of the wheel because if you did, you would already have invented it."

The future isn't necessarily a continuation of the past. Sometimes it jerks, disrupts, jolts us forward, catapults us into a new age. How can we even begin to think constructively about the time that lies ahead? The answer lies in a risk management tool called the cone of uncertainty. It is intended to illustrate that the further ahead in time we look, the less certain things become. We could just as well call it the cone of possibilities. We have no problem applying the cone when peering backwards in history, which is why the past is famously referred to as "a foreign country". Looking ahead, however, we often succumb to reductionism. The future is compressed into four megatrends, two scenarios or simply one thing, which is why we say things like "the electric car is the future." We have a tendency to close down the future and make it understandable but in doing so, we get the wrong idea. The future doesn't shrink – it expands. One job role, computer programmer, for example, becomes 15 different jobs, from Java programmer to systems architect. Take a look at Charles Darwin's illustration of how species evolve on the opposite page. One beak becomes a dozen specialized beaks. The cone of uncertainty is there to remind us to apply the same variety and richness we saw in the past to the tapestry of tomorrow.

TAKEAWAY: THE FUTURE IS RICHER, MORE DIVERSE AND MORE FRAGMENTED THAN TODAY.

SECTION TWO:
THE MOBILE PHONE AND THE FELLED TREE

Imagine the place where you live as it was 500 years ago. The buildings are gone. The people are different. Depending on where you are, there might be nothing but a lush meadow, some grazing animals and some villagers wondering about. Now stretch your imagination to see yourself time-travelling back to meet these villagers. To avoid scaring them, you have done your best to fit in by letting your body hair grow and dressing in something resembling a sack. Your goal here is to tell them about the future. There is an easy and a difficult way to do it. The easy way is to round up the locals and warn them about all the things that will disappear. The trees will be cut down, many of the wild animals become extinct and cherished beliefs will be annihilated. This is easy because we can all visualize having something and losing it.

The difficult way of telling them about the future would be to explain that, by the early 21st century, they will all have access to a shiny, new smartphone. They would not have a clue what you were talking about and no matter how many times you tried to explain the concepts of electricity, remote communication, 4G technology and the mobile internet, chances are they would consider you a lunatic and have you arrested. To imagine having something of which you have never heard, let alone needed, is abstract. A seemingly straightforward device like a mobile phone stands on top of inventions that, in turn, stand on top of other inventions making it a synthesis of knowledge from across the centuries. You don't have to travel back to the Middle Ages – a name that came much later – to see these two different ways of talking about the future in action. Today, whenever the future is discussed, it is highly likely that it is used to describe the loss of things – from clean air and a stable climate to job security and public virtue. The future thus becomes something threatening, rather than a promise of something better, no matter how abstract that improvement might be.

Mastering so-called *minus futures* – things that will disappear – is easy. This is why cinemas are full of dystopian movies like *Mad Max*, *Planet of The Apes*, *The Hunger Games* and *Divergent* where something we once had – gasoline, civilization or freedom – has been taken from us. Mastering *plus futures* – something will come along that we could never imagine – is the black belt of futurology. We tend to frown upon predictions about tripled life spans or cold fusion energy and dismiss them as mere science fiction, disconnected from reality. However, if you preoccupy your mind with minus futures, you will live in a state of constant worry. To explore what lies beyond the horizon fully, open your mind to magic.

TAKEAWAY: THE FUTURE TAKES AND THE FUTURE GIVES. ENSURE THAT YOUR THINKING IS EQUALLY MULTI-DIMENSIONAL.

SECTION THREE:
IT BEGINS WITH MAGIC

The IBM RAMAC computer in the 1950s was a beast of a machine. It weighed a tonne, had to be moved by forklift and shipped on cargo planes. The machine was a hard drive containing a mere five megabytes, which is approximately one small digital photograph. Today, we might have 50-gigabyte memory sticks attached to our key chains and the devices are usually used as free giveaways at conferences and trade shows. What was once expensive, exclusive and only for the very elite in society has become something we give away for free. This is the magic of technology. Flying used to be magic – now we do it cheaply and casually on a daily basis. Telepathy – reading other people's thoughts – used to be magic, now we call it Twitter.

To understand what the future might bring us, it is somewhat useful to start with magic, because before human beings are able to do something in the real world, we have the ability to imagine it. This is why visions of tomorrow often begin as science fiction – from the portable communication devices in *Star Trek* foreshadowing the mobile phone to Leonardo Da Vinci's aerial screw centuries before the helicopter took flight. The real world has constrictions in terms of costs and know-how but the mind can move seamlessly between the possible and the impossible. If you limit your thoughts to the logical and plausible, your predictions of tomorrow's world will not be bold enough to come true. This is why 1950s science fiction films and television series' strike us as old-fashioned today. They imagined giant tomatoes, robot housemaids, flying cars and space colonies yet failed to predict female emancipation, urbanization, lesbian, gay, bisexual and transgender (LGBT) rights and the mass-immigration and emigration of people around the planet. So even when the 1950s future families were surrounded by futuristic gadgets, they were still based on white, middle-class suburban heterosexual couples where the father was a banker and mother stayed home making cupcakes.

TAKEAWAY: THINK MAGIC – BEYOND GADGETS.

SECTION FOUR:
THE SOUNDS OF DISBELIEF

The borders that mark the cone of uncertainty are characterized by wonder, provocation, denial and disbelief. A helpful way to remember them is the four w's: "wow!", "whoa!", "what?" and "no way!" These are things we are likely to exclaim when faced with the possibilities for the future. They are also what we should demand when thoughts – our own or others' – about what lies ahead are presented. Too often, we settle for ideas that provoke a mere "hmmm", "sounds plausible" or "good idea!" The words "good idea" are particularly deceptive in that a good idea is usually what we strive to achieve but "good" ideas tend to lead us astray.

For an idea to be good it has to be comprehendible, which eliminates complex ideas. For an idea to be comprehendible, it has to be relatable to people in the present, which eliminates ideas that sound weird or unsympathetic. Finally, for an idea to earn the epithet "good", it has to sound positive and benevolent. Many ideas that turned out to have a positive impact started out sounding threatening. An example of a complex, non-relatable, threatening idea that ended up improving the lives of millions is when Doctor John Leal, a health inspector in the US, poured chlorine – a smelly, toxic chemical – into the drinking water of New Jersey. He operated like a terrorist "In almost complete secrecy, without any permission from government authorities (and no notice to the general public)", in the words of Steven Johnson's book *How We Got To Now: Six Innovations That Made the Modern World*. Miraculously the low level of chlorine disinfected the water without making people ill and has thereafter been emulated across the world, saving countless lives from deadly water-borne diseases.

TAKEAWAY: DON'T SETTLE FOR A "GOOD" IDEA WHEN WEIRD, WACKY AND WILD IDEAS ARE NEEDED TO CHANGE THE WORLD.

SECTION FIVE:
A RULE OF THUMB

A useful way to challenge oneself when thinking about the future is to assume that, for every decade that passes, <u>one</u> assumption will change or disappear. To illustrate, consider the assumptions we make about cars – that they have four wheels, run on diesel or gasoline, have a steering wheel, and so on. Now, for every decade you are looking forward, one of these assumptions will change or disappear completely so that half a century hence, the car may have three wheels, run on electricity and be without a steering wheel. With the car being a common object of our future fantasizing, these changes may not sound particularly groundbreaking. Imagine thinking about buildings instead. A building has walls, doors, windows and is an immoveable object in which we either live, work or store things. When these assumptions change over the coming decades, a building might not be immovable anymore but migrate and it may be used for vertical farming or some new, as yet unknown, purpose.

The rule of changing assumptions applies to all aspects of life. Our marriages will lose the passionate love that signifies newlyweds to become relationships characterised by friendly companionship. No matter how many children you have living at home with you today, they will – hopefully – all move out in the coming few decades. The objective here is not necessarily to predict accurately what a Tuesday afternoon in the year 2066 will look like but to use the cone of uncertainty as kind of mind-altering drug. When you get better at it, you can start to play around with thrilling visions like the following, which was shared at a recent TED conference: "The next Einstein has already been born but she is a computer programmer."

When exploring the great beyond, it's important not just to dwell on what tomorrow will *look* like. The flying car is an overused symbol of the future because it simply bolts on wings to a well-known object making it easy for us to visualize. But tomorrow will be immersive – full of sounds, feelings and smells, many as yet unheard, unfelt and unknown. What are the dimensions of your personality with which you have – for better or worse – not yet come into contact? What are the feelings for which we have no names? Where might the nameless streets that U2 sing of lead us? The future is an enigma to be filled with our dreams and desires, something that requires us to be constructively imaginative. The next section will teach us constructive imagination by organizing time into different dimensions.

TAKEAWAY: WHEN USED WELL, THE CONE OF UNCERTAINTY HAS THE SAME PROPERTIES AS A MIND-ALTERING DRUG.

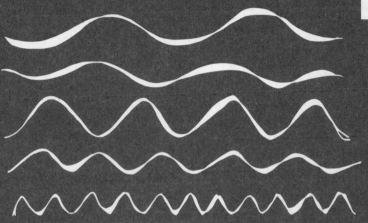

PART THREE

THINK IN
PACE LAYERS!

SECTION ONE:
A CITY STROLL

Change has several gears and variable speeds, which is obvious when you walk on a busy city street. At street level, you see people and hear the sounds of voices and engines. This is where changes are quick – the fashion we wear, gadgets we use and cars we drive change yearly or even monthly. If you stop and move your eyes fractionally upwards to the facades of the buildings, you will see logotypes announcing what shop or office is occupying the building. The fortunes of the tenants rise and fall along slower currents with booms and busts happening every five-to-10 years. You take a few steps back to see the building in its entirety. Architecture and infrastructure reflects governance, cultural-shifts and technological development that move on multi-decade trajectories. Finally, you hop into a spaceship or log on to Google Earth to gaze down at our planet from space. You see prickles of lights interspersed with general darkness reflecting urbanization, types of energy use and other developments that take place across centuries.

Like the age rings on a tree, these layers of change reveal that time is indeed relative. When a fashion designer talks about "the future", he or she will mean the autumn season next year whereas an architect or city planner will use the word to denote a point in time several decades ahead of us. Similarly, even though your future begins in a few minutes, you will need to use different kinds of planning tools depending on whether you are planning for a dinner party tomorrow night or your own retirement 20 years hence. Be warned, however, that the human brain is significantly skewed towards the here and now.

TAKEAWAY: THERE ARE FOUR SHADES OF "THEN" – FROM THE QUICK, FASHION CHANGES ON THE STREET TO THE CENTURY-LONG CHANGES WE CAN ONLY SEE FROM SPACE.

SECTION TWO:
FROM MICROTRENDS TO GIGATRENDS

The time needed to a change a shirt or download a new app is less than a minute. This is why many of the things we humans do, wear or use can be characterized as *microtrends*. The word "trend" has its etymological origin in the Norse word *trendr* – to turn – but has come to mean a current, flow and common direction in observations. Microtrends have become significantly easier to track with the rise of social media. For a company that sells fashion – and this includes many technology, travel and lifestyle companies today, not just garment manufacturers – tracking and adapting to microtrends has become a key survival strategy, albeit a risky one; risky because taste is fickle and following a microtrend too far means a warm embrace by the consumer one season leaves you stranded out in the cold the next.

Macrotrends are what we saw in the city stroll when looking at which companies had their names on buildings, reflecting the rise and fall of various firms and industries. These fortunes tend to correlate with the business cycles – boom and bust, spend and save – that are invisible yet powerful forces in society. The economy can be likened to appetite and we all know the feeling of eating like there is no tomorrow – boom – only to find ourselves with belt unbuckled on the couch proclaiming that we will never eat again – bust. The past few decades have, however, seen a new kind of boom that can be more likened to a mass hysteria. We had a dot.com boom in the late 1990s when everyone wanted to own stock in, and work for, a new breed of online companies. A global credit boom followed wherein borrowing money was cheap, real estate soared and banks made money from increasingly opaque products. Each boom ended not with a fizzle but with a collapse in the global economy. There seemed to be some kind of pied piper luring everyone – regardless of actual appetite – towards an abyss masquerading as a Shangri-La. In other words, tracking macrotrends has become significantly more difficult, which is why finance ministers and chief economists alike have overused the word "unpredictable."

Third, we were able to see megatrends when we took a step back to see what the city buildings were made of and looked like. Architecture is a blend of technological capabilities, societal aspirations and aesthetic preferences. It is, in the words of the composer Richard Wagner, a *gesamtkunstwerk* (a "total work of art"). This is why we can pinpoint the exact moment when glass became cheaper and easier to sculpt since virtually every building in the late 1980s is bound to have high glass walls or glass roofs. Similarly, the rise of oriel windows, the iconic balcony-like structures that protrude from buildings, reflects urbanization movements where space becomes dearer and people want to create extra space without using more land. The most long-lived, successful companies in the world built their business with megatrends in mind. Take IKEA, the Swedish furniture store that set out in the 1950s to furnish the homes of the middle-classes, using the slogan "a better everyday life for the many people". It has since followed the rise of the middle classes across Europe, the US and Asia.

Finally, the gigatrends we saw when gazing down on Earth from space are the turtle-paced movements that change the human condition at its core. We have names for some of them – The Dark Ages, The Enlightenment – but the names were added much later by which time we had gained a perspective on what a certain century meant. Most often, we don't see or understand what we are in the middle of, just as fish, famously, do not "discover" water. Sometimes, the most difficult thing to predict is the present. Gigatrends create a particular kind of future-thinking where we first have to go forward in time to understand where we are right now. Therefore, a gigatrend tends to be more of a philosophical tool – where are we and what is this all pointing to? – than a map.

TAKEAWAY: WANT TO MAKE A FAST BUCK? THINK MICROTRENDS. WANT TO CHANGE THE WORLD? THINK GIGATRENDS.

SECTION THREE:
THE OBLIVIOUS BRAIN

Surrounded by these rich layers of time – from the vividly colourful microtrends to the silent-but-powerful gigatrends – you would think that the brain would have developed a multidimensional scanning system. This is unfortunately not the case. Instead, the brain spends most of its energy on the here and now. Our five senses are exclusively focused on the present. The sixth sense remains a fantasy. An oft-cited study shows that we, on average, spend a mere 12% of a day thinking about the future, with the remaining time spent reacting to surrounding stimuli. The future is a daydream – an aspiration – when our days have been reduced to a list of things that should have been done yesterday.

Our brains are wired for the present because that's how prehistoric man survived. He did not have to face invisible challenges like carbon dioxide emissions, high levels of cholesterol or mortgage payments. Most challenges we face today are connected to threats that loom across decades, even centuries. In other words, our survival mechanism has become an annihilation machine where "now" is an enemy of "then". If we divide everything we do into either present-intense activities or future-intense activities, we can see this conflict clearly. Enjoying a large slice of key lime pie – yum! Sweating at the gym – eurgh! Splurging on a really nice pair of shoes - yes! Putting away some money for a rainy day – yawn! Flying somewhere nice for holiday – cool! Staying at home when everyone else goes somewhere nice for vacation – uncool!

Present-intense activities feel good whereas future-intense activities feel underwhelming, if they can be felt at all. Yet our long-term wellbeing is dependent on our ability to sacrifice "yum", "yes" and "cool" for "ergh", "yawn" and "uncool". This is why Aristotle divided happiness into hedonism - realizing the fulfilment of pleasure – and eudaimonism, striving towards long-term happiness or literally "having a good guardian spirit." We tend to teleport things from the eudaimonic realm to the hedonic. We borrow money from our future selves because we think we might need it more today. When we drink alcohol, we teleport energy from Saturday morning to Friday night in order to get an extra jolt on the dance floor or for socialising at the bar. Teleportation often leaves us with a hangover.

TAKEAWAY: THE FUTURE WILL REQUIRE US TO SACRIFICE THE NOW ON THE ALTAR OF THE THEN.

SECTION FOUR:
INFORMATION DIETS

The way to break out of the feel-good prison of the present is not by convincing yourself that kale tastes better than candy. Self-deception will only lead to resentment. What you need to change is your information diet – the things with which you feed your head. We tend to surround ourselves with news - from Al Jazeera broadcasts to social media gossip. With today's superconnected media channels, news should be called "nows" because it deals almost exclusively with real-time events. What it gains in speed, it sacrifices in accuracy. Yet our brain doesn't have a built-in bullshit detector that homes in on truths and makes us vomit blood when we hear a lie. In fact, we even prefer sexy lies to boring truths. Take the number pi – 3.14 - for example. Few people are able to recite it to more than two decimal places, yet pi is a very useful number with which we can build houses and programme space shuttles. Celebrity rehab stints or the philandering of a royal family member, on the other hand, is completely useless information yet more people read gossip magazines in their spare time than memorize 3.14159265. This is because information is a social currency. Try reciting pi at a cocktail reception versus making up something juicy and sensational about Celebrity X or Acquaintance Y. One will leave people scurrying for the exit – the other will make you Queen of the party. Our brain prefers sexy lies to boring truths. Infobesity happens when our brains are full of junk: news, gossip and lies.

A balanced information diet requires inconvenient truths, complexity, ambiguity and information that might make no sense today but might someday in the distant future. A school is a beautiful mechanism for curing infobesity, which is why in this time of digital tablets, personal entertainment and internet gluttony, schools should strive to become even more boring. Boredom pays off in the long run.

TAKEAWAY: FEEL GOOD OR THINK RIGHT?

SECTION FIVE:
INFLECTION POINTS

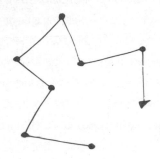

Why can the world economy seem to be flourishing only to collapse over night? How come a long peace is shattered by a single assassin's bullet? Why does a lifelong marriage end suddenly? The word "trend" leads us astray into seeing changes as linear and predictable. The reality is that trends are like a messy plate of spaghetti – they intertwine, twist and break off. We want to see our lives as trajectories – stories where we, the protagonist, have some particular end goal and destination waiting for us. Yet we might be the antagonists in somebody else's story. Or perhaps it's not a story at all but real life with all its injustices, peculiarities and mysteries. What happens when our long, stable narrative threads rapidly change direction and our lives derail?

With hindsight, everything becomes clear. Al Qaeda did not begin its operations on September 11, 2001 but had been building a network and organizing attacks for a decade. The man or woman of your dreams had been leaving you for years when he or she walked out on that fateful night. The butterfly had been a caterpillar and a cocoon before it spread its wings. Because the brain is primarily built for the present, we extrapolate the present moment and assume now will last forever – our babies will always require diapers, our bodies will always stay strong and our current misfortune is a lifelong curse. When change happens, our instinct is disbelief. We don't accept what is happening and consider it a dream or a nightmare. The feeling of disbelief is usually followed by feelings – anger, sadness or joy depending on what just happened. Acceptance and understanding come later.

Elisabeth Kuebler-Ross outlined the phases we go through when faced with a terminal illness by coining the acronym DABDA: denial, anger, bargaining, depression and acceptance. These can be modified and applied to a more general reaction to drastic change: DEDI - disbelief, euphoria, disillusionment and invisibility. Take the invention of the World Wide Web. Our first weary steps on the information superhighway in the early 1990s were interspersed with "amazing!" and "wow!" Then came the Euphoria where the web would change everything and make geography redundant. This was replaced by mass-bankruptcies and stock market meltdown where we wandered the digital ruins in search of what went wrong. Finally, the internet has become an invisible force we take for granted, just like electricity.

TAKEWAY: THE FUTURE IS NOT SMOOTH BUT JAGGED, DISCONTINUOUS AND FULL OF "OOHS", "AHHS" AND "HA-HAS"

SECTION SIX:
THE VALUE OF
PROVOCATION

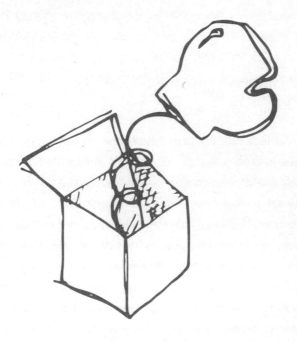

Adults tend to believe that the world is more or less like when they were growing up and that everything happening in the world right now is an exception to this norm. In fact, you can even claim that ageing hardens your values and opinions into dogma. The child is curious and open-minded. Some of the elderly are wise but many have become rigid, bitter and complain that the world of yesteryear is no more. Part of this process is brain chemistry. The first kiss is bound to be a whirlwind of emotions whereas the 8.000th kiss will be more of a breeze. The brain packages new experiences as memories that we can access making the world over time more familiar even though there is still an infinite number of new experiences to try. The problem is that a new experience isn't necessarily a pleasant endeavour. New kinds of art can provoke feelings of disgust, even hostility. New kinds of food may taste strange. Sleeping with a new partner can create all kinds of problems, especially if you are in a relationship with someone else.

We live our lives with the convenient delusion that everything has already been invented and most things are as they should be. When somebody challenges the present, the status quo will fight to keep its status. Yet it is in the new that we encounter the future – be it art, music, sexuality, lifestyles. The new may offend us but make future generations grateful. Homosexuality was, for a long time, treated as a crime but is now something celebrated in pride parades and, according to research, a prerequisite for a city to become a haven of innovation. This is why censorship is so detrimental. Not only because it punishes the creator but also us consumers. We are forced to wallow in the circles of the present instead of enjoying the thrills of the roller-coaster ride that tomorrow can bring. Trends are thinking-tools to help us compartmentalize time and distinguish between the things that change fast and slow. These are not forces of nature, however, but man-made and triggered by a lonely, visionary genius. Some are evil. Others are the guardian angels of the future.

TAKEAWAY: SEEK TO HAVE THE MIND OF A CHILD. EMBRACE THE THRILL OF THE NEW.

_____

_____

_____

_____

_____

_____

_____

_____

_____

_____

_____

_____

PART FOUR

DISTINGUISH BETWEEN HORIZONTAL AND VERTICAL CHANGE

SECTION ONE:
A CITY STROLL
REVISITED

Imagine, once again, that you are walking in a city. Surrounding you are modern skyscrapers with contemporary brands advertised on giant LED screens. People are walking briskly, dressed for business, most with a smartphone in one hand and a takeaway coffee cup in the other. Parked along the kerb of the busy street are sleek premium cars from around the world. You get the picture. But what city are you imagining? A couple of decades ago, the description would have fit only a handful of places, such as New York, Hong Kong and Tokyo. Today, there are more than 100 cities that have skyscrapers, a vibrant business climate, BMWs, chain coffee bars and so on.

We have seen the emergence of a world where the exact same thing is happening in more and more places. This is an example of *horizontal change* – things, ideas, people and inventions being copied and pasted around the world. This is why we encounter Californian technology, German Cars, Sushi bars serving French wines and Asian hotel chains wherever we travel today. To come up with an idea that is globally unique in a world of horizontal change is very difficult but a locally unique idea is easy. If you want to create a ground-breaking idea in a place near you, all you have to do is R&D – rip-off and duplicate. Simply go to Silicon Valley or some other innovative place and bring back whatever you find there – be it a new yoga style, a new type of culsIne or a piece of technology. Because change comes later to some parts of the world, the idea that you ripped off and duplicated will be considered fresh and different when you take it from California to Sweden, Slovenia or Switzerland. Similarly, whatever problem you are facing, somebody is bound to have solved it somewhere already especially if the problem is connected to some universal human emotion like love, loneliness, sadness or fear.

TAKEAWAY: DON'T START WITH A WHITE SHEET OF PAPER TO GET IDEAS, START WITH A PLANE TICKET OR A SEARCH ENGINE TO RIP OFF AND DUPLICATE.

SECTION TWO:
WHEN DIVERSITY TURNS TO SAMENESS

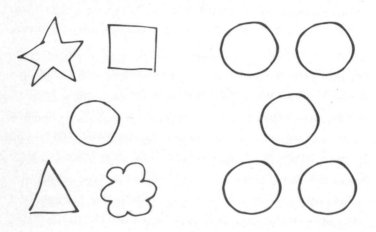

The 1959 Cadillac Eldorado with its iconic tail fins and long, surfboard-like chassis comes from a time in history when cars were really different from one another. Nobody would mistake the Eldorado for a Volvo PV544 or a Mercedes Benz 190 SL from the same year. Diversity was the norm in automobiles. Similarly, the mobile phones we used in the 1990s were highly differentiated in terms of size, colour, functionality and ring tone. Or think about a nursery full of children – different in how they dress, spontaneous in how they play with varying levels of maturity and behaviour. It seems as if things start out in states of great variety – from people to cars and cell phones.

Fast forward, however, and you end up with sameness. Distinguishing car brands in a traffic jam today has become extremely difficult with most makers offering some version of a fuel-efficient, compact mini-SUV. Cell phones have become a jungle of identical black blocks of touchscreen glass. And the children at nursery have grown up to become identically dressed management consultants, bankers or accountants.

Diversity transformed into sameness. Why? Because ripping off and duplicating is easier than trailblazing, pioneering and exploring. This is known as *Hotelling's Law* or "the principle of minimum differentiation" in economics. It explains how it is rational for producers to make their products and offerings as similar as possible to minimize risks and maximize the potential number of customers. This is why markets – whether for cars, gadgets or dating apps – are characterized by increasing competition over time. Not just markets, but our lives too. Want to get into a good school? Competition. Want to work for an attractive employer? Competition. This leads to the kind of status anxiety that characterizes modern lives, where people strive to live in a certain neighbourhood, in a certain kind of house with a specific set of lifestyle attributes. Competition is the outcome in a world where change is primarily horizontal, and we are all left scurrying to get a piece of the same pie.

TAKEAWAY: WE ARE CAPABLE OF UNIQUENESS BUT SUCCUMB TO SAMENESS OVER TIME.

SECTION THREE:
THE CASUALTIES
OF COMPETITION

Finding happiness is a mystery. Finding unhappiness is relatively straightforward. If you want to be unhappy, just compare yourself to someone else. No matter how self-confident you feel, there's always someone thinner, richer, smarter, nicer or more successful. Similarly, companies that dwell on competition too much tend to lose a lot of things that made them successful in the first place – their ideas, courage and risk-willingness; in short, their *chutzpah*. Amazon's founder Jeff Bezos urges his company to avoid wasting time thinking about the competitors because "they will never give us any money". This doesn't stop others from speaking about a hyper-competitive market, a levelled playing field, a battle for position, and a war for talent.

You know you work for a company that is dwelling on competition when it uses sports metaphors to describe the future. This is a common phenomenon today. Managers are urged to "play as a team", "play to win" and markets are jolted by "gamechangers." Sports personalities are paid well for giving motivational talks about setting goals and working hard. Companies even sponsor sports teams and competitions to send the message that they too are on a winning streak. Sport is a seductive metaphor for the abstract world of modern business yet it is completely misleading.

First, competitive sports rely on a certain element of luck. This is known in sports psychology as the paradox of skill. When athletes are of equal skill, luck often determines the outcome, which is why results are often the outcome of a referee's call, a millisecond at the finish line or a key player becoming injured at a crucial point in the game. Luck is a key ingredient in sports but should not be counted on in business. It doesn't build airplanes, cure diseases or enable people to send text messages around the world for free. Luck – in the sense of being in the right place at the right time – may shift the fortune for a business but should as far as possible be taken out of the equation when we plan for the future.

Similarly, we cannot live in a world where people are slaves to their own luck or lack thereof. This is why we have social safety nets and insurance, so that people can live decent lives regardless of the cards they have been dealt (pardon the games metaphor). The second reason sport metaphors mislead us is that rules don't change in the middle of a game yet they have a nasty habit of changing all the time in business, from government regulation to the "rules" of what consumers want and the frontier of technological capability. Sports metaphors should therefore be avoided at all costs in companies. And in our lives too.

TAKEAWAY: COMPARISON IS THE THIEF OF ALL JOY. COMPETITION IS THE THIEF OF BIG IDEAS.

SECTION FOUR:
WHEN THE FUTURE BEGAN

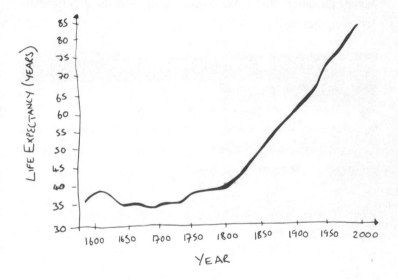

The future begins as magic – whether it's flying, curing a fatal disease or the telepathy enabled by Twitter. When the science fiction author William Gibson famously said that "the future is already here — it's just not very evenly distributed", he was referring to horizontal change, not the magic of *vertical change*. Vertical change happens when something previously impossible, even unfathomable, becomes a reality. It may begin in the head of a genius that others call a madman, or in a laboratory, or in an experiment. It is painful, disruptive and messy yet completely necessary for the world to progress to a new level of wellbeing and prosperity.

Take a look at the diagram above. We see that life expectancy was, for centuries, stagnant – even declining – reflecting a society that was fundamentally cyclical and unchanging in nature. Our children's lives would be as short – even shorter – than ours. The jobs they took, the tools they owned, where they lived and who they married were identical to the jobs, tools and lives of previous generations. There were many downsides and one significant upside: in an unchanging world, those in power would enjoy a monopoly for centuries. Whether you were a mason making keystones, a monk writing books by hand or a farming peasant, you could trust that your trade would be passed on unchanged through generations.

At the inflection point of the diagram around the year 1800, things start to change. Instead of blindly trusting our elders, we started using our eyes and a scientific revolution was born. It made the world healthier, wealthier and all the other good things you have heard Professor Hans Rosling speak about in his world-renowned TED talks. There are many upsides to living in a progressively changing world and one significant downside. In a world that changes, every idea has a "best before" date. Take pensions, for example, which were thought up in Germany in the late 1880s. Chancellor Bismarck stipulated that Germans who managed to reach the age of 70 should be allowed to retire. Life expectancy, as you can see in the diagram, was at the time approximately 55. Had The Iron Chancellor invented pensions in

2005, he would have insisted on Germans retiring when they turned 106. In a world in which more of us live longer, retiring before age 60 or 70 is out of sync with reality.

Similarly, marriage was, for decades, simply a judicial contract to protect property. With the rise of Romanticism in the early 1800s came the idea that matrimony should be for love, primarily, not legal necessity. The modern wedding ceremony wherein you promise to love someone forever was born at this time and, of course, promising to love someone forever with a life expectancy of 50 Is not particularly difficult. The rise of divorce, new kinds of relationships and swinging clubs were born in correlation with a rise in life expectancy. The future, like a battery, has a plus and a minus. Some things – longer, healthier lives – are gained while we are forced to let go of others, like lifelong marriages and job security.

TAKEAWAY: THE FUTURE BEGINS WHEN WE LET GO OF THE PAST.

SECTION FIVE:
SHARKS AND SKEUOMORPHS

Sharks swam with the dinosaurs. The creatures are more than 400 million years old and have evolved to a state of near perfection. If evolution is about the survival of the fittest, there is no creature in the food chain better at being a shark than a shark. Similarly, the book has technically remained the same for centuries (pages of paper in between a cover) just like beer – fermented malt juice – and barbecues – cooking a dead animal over an open fire. We often make the erroneous assumption that *everything* will change in the future thereby disregarding the many "sharks" surrounding us.

The opposite of a shark is a *skeuomorph* – an archaic idea about what something should look like. The best examples of skeuomorphs are the icons in your computer programs. If you gave a 3.5 inch floppy disk to a child today, he or she would assume you had 3D-printed the save button in Microsoft Word. The symbol for movies in iTunes looks like a bunk-bed to him or her. We even refer to movies as "films", another skeuomorph where the celluloid plastic film on which movies used to be printed is used as a symbol of an entertainment art form that is today spread using digital binary digits. We measure engine strength in "horse power" and the wheel width of a car corresponds to standards that were set out by Roman chariots, thousands of years ago. Skeumorphs remain in our midst, leaving a residue of the past on the fabric of the present. At best, they are pedagogic artefacts that enable us to operate our computers more efficiently or create a standard for talking about movies or car engines. At worst, they create a "wrongium" price for us to pay.

A "premium" is the extra money we are willing to pay because we value something – from designer handbags to three star restaurants. Wrongium is the extra price we pay because an area is skeuomorph-ridden. One example is the lack of information in retailing, meaning that stores have to guess what consumers want, thereby having to throw away or sell the inventory at a significant markdown. The money lost is the wrongium. Similarly, business academics talk about a "strategy tax" that arises when companies turn down future opportunities to optimize and focus their current business. Kodak paid a strategy tax when it failed to invent Instagram. Nokia paid a strategy tax when it failed to launch the iPhone. The strategy tax is the price you pay for following a certain path and disregarding others that turned out to have more potential in the future.

Wrongium and strategy tax also exist on an individual level. The bitterness and resentment felt by a recent divorcee could be equated to a kind of wrongium and the turning down of all the other partners they could have met but did not, in order to stay faithful, represent a kind of emotional strategy tax. Yet people pride themselves on fidelity and long relationships so we should not berate individuals or organizations too much for having the courage to follow a specific path when there were so many to choose from. This, after all, is what leadership is all about.

TAKEAWAY: THE GRAVITATIONAL PULL OF THE PAST MEANS WE PAY AN INVISIBLE PRICE WHEN WE CLING TO IT.

SECTION SIX:
DO WHAT OTHERS DO OR DO SOMETHING NEW
(HEY, AN EIGHT WORD POEM!)

Our lives move on a horizontal or vertical trajectory. Most of the time, we are guided by the choices of others – we study what others have studied, pursue jobs that others have pursued, move to the city where others already live and so on. Then, all of a sudden, a path to a life less ordinary opens up. Maybe we are fired from our job and see it as a change catalyst. Maybe the city transforms us into someone we didn't set out to be and our unfamiliar reflection in the mirror beckons us to move away. An unexpected encounter. A dream you can't shake.

These are all epiphanies that can take us from the sameness of horizontal living to the unchartered territory of living vertically.

The people we admire most tend to be those who responded to the epiphany and did something that no-one had done before. Yet we have a tendency to strive for a life of comfort and convenience. What if the new path is risky? We model our risks based on the experiences of others so, naturally, we stay away from endeavours at which others have failed. Risk, however, is a measurement of probability – what is the likelihood that something will happen again? Vertical living, by definition, has no precedents and cannot be modelled. Sure, you can control for some factors but by doing so risk falling into the narrative trap where you evaluate options based on whether they sound good or not. Paul Gauguin abandoned his wife and five children to devote his life to painting in Tahiti. The toll it took on his family is incalculable but his unique art made him a legend, posthumously. Vertical living is no walk in the park. It will force you to do tough trade-offs where the costs are immediate but the returns absent for decades. Just imagine the number of pioneers who died lonely, dirt-poor and broken only to be rediscovered long after their death. When it comes to choosing what path to take in life, a useful principle to guide you is as follows:

If you are planning to do something already done by somebody else, start by asking him or her about it. The best model we have for determining outcomes is to ask those who already chose the path we are planning, whether we are talking about going to business school, cheating on our spouse, starting a company or undergoing chemotherapy.

If you are planning to do something where you cannot find anyone who has taken that path, follow the slogan of a famous sports brand and just do it. If you fail, you will learn. If you succeed, you will become a hero for the rest of us stuck in the shackles of a horizontal life we ripped off and duplicated from somebody else.

TAKEAWAY: DARE TO LIVE VERTICALLY. YOU WILL NOT REGRET IT.

SECTION SEVEN:
A HORIZONTAL OR VERTICAL WORLD?

"History is a wheel, for the nature of man is fundamentally unchanging. What has happened before will perforce happen again." These are words spoken in the world of *Game of Thrones*, a series of books turned into a TV-series. It is a description not only of the fantasy world in which the books take place but also of the world we used to inhabit. Rewind time a few hundred years and society was pegged to a cyclical wheel – we really could not make new things, so wealth and power would have to be taken from others, often through bloody means. We still succumb to this kind of zero-sum mindset. The words "developing countries" and "developed countries" imply that some places are done evolving and others aspire to become like them. Globalization is often described as a kind of tournament in which nations win over others in the sports of educational results, exports, quality of life or patents filed; as if the fortune of one country happens at the expense of another. To see the world as unchanging is easy. To see the world for what it could be is the difficult part. Hollywood has trained us for years to envision the future as a dystopian, post-apocalyptic war zone so to imagine what new miracles lie beyond the horizon becomes the big challenge we face. To compete – jostle for money, fame and success – is easy. To create – go where others fear to tread and bring a new idea into this world – is difficult. If we want to live in a world that breaks the wheel, somebody somewhere will need to create.

Ignaz Semmelweis, a Hungarian physician, had the radical idea in the mid-1800s that if doctors in hospitals were to wash their hands regularly, fewer patients would die. He was met by scepticism and ridicule. It would take him more than two decades to champion the cause, but when he finally succeeded, he was suffering from mental illness, possibly accelerated from the constant torment of the medical community, and he died in an Austrian mental asylum, aged 47.

We live in a world in which those who create are often rejected while those who compete successfully are celebrated as heroes. We make sports stars our national ambassadors. We put good looking business people on magazine covers. We give scholarships to students with high grades. The person with the audacity to challenge our world is rejected, unless they succeed; in other words, prove to be competitive. We have a propensity to compete, not create. Yet the future is dependent on the human ability to make something new. We will see in Part Five just why creation is so controversial.

TAKEAWAY: CREATION, LIKE GOLD, IS RARE, DIFFICULT TO OBTAIN AND VERY VALUABLE.

PART FIVE

A LANDSCAPE
OF MOUNTAINS,
NOT STRAIGHT
LINES

SECTION ONE:
NOW IS FOREVER

When we find ourselves in blissful conditions – sipping a glass of chilled white wine while watching a sunset by the ocean – we often wish that the moment would last forever. In statistics, such wishful thinking is called extrapolation – or stretching the present into the future. We hear economists talk about China in the year 2050 based on current growth or ecologists warning about the depletion of resources because of current overuse. US singer/songwriter Bryan Adams even recorded a song called *18 till I die* about the kind of extrapolation we all apply to our lives, not just wishing but actually feeling as if we are a certain age until our bodies, or hopelessly out-of-date dancing styles, tell us otherwise. Extrapolation leads us off course. If we apply the economist's mathematics of China to children, they will be more than metres tall and weigh 12 tonnes each, based on current growth.

Yet we are prone to draw straight lines into the future – we even refer to a "timeline" when pinpointing certain places behind or ahead of us – when what we should be seeing is a mountain range, a landscape of peaks and troughs where we can move across many dimensions, not just up or down on a two-dimensional arrow. It's useful to think about mobility to make the mountain metaphor easier to grasp. Human beings began by walking and running to get around. We can call it "Legs Mountain". Then we found another mountaintop that we can call "Horse Mountain" wherein horses, donkeys and in some places camels and elephants were used to get around quicker. Just next to Horse Mountain was "Carriage Peak" where we added wheeled wagons to the horses in order to facilitate the moving of people and goods. Further ahead, by the horizon, lay "Automobile Mountain" that we began climbing in the late 1890s and are still climbing to date. By viewing mobility as mountains, we see that progress is discontinuous. We climb up one mountain and reach the peak where the extent of what we can accomplish by walking and running has been exhausted.

We therefore have to climb down and move sideways before we can climb up the next mountain. At the time of writing this, in 2015, it is unclear if Automobile Mountain can take us any further with emissions-heavy, noisy vehicles standing either unused or in gridlocked traffic in cities around the world. Perhaps we need to climb down again and see where Bicycle Mountain can take us? This is why creation is so controversial. It destroys before it creates. To reach higher, we first have to admit we are on the wrong mountain, then climb down, move sideways and then climb up again.

We can apply the mountain metaphor to happiness. Once upon a time, happiness was a binary outcome usually based on your relationship to God or another deity. If you prayed and behaved well, happiness was yours. The sinner would remain unhappy. Then came psychoanalysis wherein happiness – or lack thereof - was connected to various experiences in life, especially in childhood. When we started to map the human brain, we saw that emotional experiences are connected to neurochemicals and were able to alter our moods medically. For every shift that happened in our understanding of happiness, power was taken from some and given to others as two truths cannot coexist and be equally valid. Priests, psychoanalysts and pharmaceutical companies still argue about what *really* makes us happy. Happiness – once a top-down, religious system of which we were subordinates – has become a landscape for us to explore on an individual level. Some connect their own wellbeing to religion, while others need drugs to be happy. Some of us find happiness over long stretches of time while others might only experience it in 10-minute bursts. By seeing things through the metaphor of the mountain landscape, we enrich our view of what is possible.

TAKEAWAY: YOU MAY BE ON THE WRONG MOUNTAIN.

SECTION TWO:
TRIGGERING CREATION

When artist Vincent Van Gogh arrived in Provence, France, in the late 1800s, he was struck not only by the beauty of the landscape but by the observation that no other artist had done justice to the "ever-changing beauty" of the area. "Good Lord, I have seen things by certain painters, and by myself too, which did not do justice to the subject at all...So there is still plenty for me to work on here," he wrote in a letter to a friend.

More than a century later, director Quentin Tarantino was having lunch with fellow filmmaker Luc Besson. Tarantino had just experienced his first failure with the box office flop *Death Proof*. He had now planned to take a step back from the silver screen and release his next project – *Inglourious Basterds* (sic) – as a TV series. Most people with whom he had shared the plan complimented him and said it was the right way forward. Besson, being a contrarian Frenchman, stayed silent and then said: "You're one of the few directors that I actually like to leave the house for, to go and see your movies at the theatres. And now you're telling me I'm going to have to wait years to do that? I'm a little disappointed." Tarantino refers to this moment as a pivotal moment: "You can't unhear it…it was running around in my head. So I said, 'Let me try and turn this into a movie one more time'." He did, and the movie became one of Tarantino's finest accomplishments artistically and biggest commercial successes.

Van Gogh and Tarantino both experienced the trigger point of creation. It is not so much a vision of the future as an insight about the present and a painful one at that: we are wrong. The assumptions made, the current way of doing things and, most damningly, the current future plans are all wrong. Few things are as painful for us as having to admit we are wrong. It may force us to accept defeat and realize we have wasted years barking up the wrong tree or, to avoid mixing metaphors, climbing the wrong mountain. Admitting we are wrong is relatively easy, though painful, on an individual level but it is near impossible on a group level. Organizations and societies may very well have realized the path they are on is unsustainable but there is too much invested in the present so they stick to routines, strategies and values even though they see another world opening up ahead of them. They promise ever higher results even though the assumptions are wrong. This is why companies die a lot sooner than humans. The individual jumps ship, brushes himself off and sets off to explore the next mountain. The company, lacking a reverse gear, remains stranded as the tide moves out like a Noah's Ark on a hilltop, that was once surrounded by life-giving water but is now a barren wasteland.

TAKEAWAY: BEING WRONG IS A PORTAL TO THE FUTURE.

SECTION THREE:
COMPETE HORIZONTALLY OR CREATE VERTICALLY?

How long do you need to work to earn <u>one hour</u> of reading light?

Year 1800
6 HOURS

Year 1880
15 MINUTES

Year 1950
8 SECONDS

Year 2015
½ SECOND

This diagram beautifully suggests that progress – creating a better world – is best measured in time, not money. The 19th century worker needed to toil away for the greater part of a work day to earn an hour of candlelight, that she was then too tired to use for the purpose of reading. Today, we spend almost no time at all to earn an hour of LED-light meaning that we have been liberated to use five hours, 59 minutes, 59.5 seconds to read, think or procrastinate. The quest of creation is a liberation movement where we seek to free ourselves from current constrictions. This sounds straightforward until you consider interests vested in the status quo. Imagine the 19th century candle maker conferences and trade shows. Imagine the candle makers whose livelihoods depended on the sale of candles. Imagine the political system being somewhat skewed to promote the exports of candle wax, let alone the sales tax earned on the current system.

The new, new thing doesn't arrive as a set industry providing safe jobs and taxable income. It begins as a technical trick – look what we can do when we dip a wick into kerosene! Nowhere is it obvious that the trick will become an industry so it quickly becomes a threat, not a promise. There is a sense of group cohesion – togetherness – in the status quo whereas the new path looks lonely. Competition is, by definition, a group activity – the Latin origin *com petare* even means to strive together – which is why we prefer competing horizontally to creating vertically. Decades later, candles had been transformed into a niche industry of mood enhancers and seduction tools with the kerosene lamp as the new normal. Then the idyllic collectivism of the industry is shattered once again by the electric light bulb. And on it goes. The future is discontinuous meaning that the knowledge and skill sets we acquire in one era become worthless in the next. Everything we know today is wrong in the future. We should strive to unlearn – erasing the old – before we learn. The creator must dare to live in a bewildered state of ambivalence and uncertainty avoiding the warm, embracing convenience of conviction. It is easier for a sceptic to shake off old assumptions than for a strong believer to let go of all the things that made him great. In the words of Roman Emperor Marcus Aurelius: "The object of life is not to be on the side of the majority, but to escape finding oneself in the ranks of the insane."

TAKEAWAY: CREATION IS A SOLO ENDEAVOUR.

PART SIX

CREATING THE FUTURE

SECTION ONE:
K*NO*WING

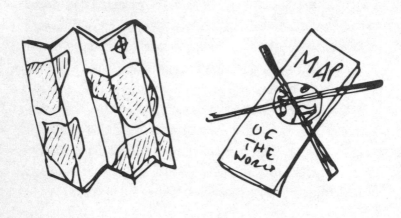

Should we live our lives according to plans and principles or should we just wing it?

Sometimes we revel in not knowing the future and proudly exclaim things such as, "let's see where tonight takes us!" At other times, we urge people to stick to fundamental ideas in the face of turbulent change and when they do, we reward them with compliments of "courage" and "integrity." Even though our rational halves understand that there is no such thing as a crystal orb through which the future reveals itself, we pay good money to mutual fund managers and tarot card readers who claim they can read our fortune. What is the learning here? Should we strive to know or not know? Should we live as if life is on rails or a blank slate? As any diligent PhD student would tell you, the answer is: "It depends."

Polish poet and Nobel laureate Wislawa Szymborska once said, "whatever inspiration is, it is born from a continuous 'I don't know.'" Another poet, John Keats, called for a "negative capability" where we seek to be "capable of being in uncertainties, mysteries, doubts, without any irritable reaching after fact and reason." When we want to open our minds to new impressions, we should switch off our instinct to know. Take the career of Björn Borg, the Swedish tennis player, as an example. He discovered the sport at an early age, and for 20 years that was all he focused on, winning several Grand Slam titles. He retired before the age of 30. Several failed business ventures followed forcing him to try to sell his many tennis trophies in the early 2000s.

Even though we admire the single-mindedness of athletes who spend all their waking hours on tennis courts or football fields, it is a risky strategy because it narrows their life options and many former sports stars succumb to depression when their short career window closes. Alfred de Musset gave excellent advice in a sonnet to Victor Hugo:" In this low life, you should love many things, in order to know at the end the things you love best." The opposite of having a Björn Borg career is having a Mastermind career. In this famous board game, one player seeks to guess the correct sequence of four coloured pegs while the other will only tell you that some guesses are wrong and others right, without being specific. It becomes a kind of experimental guessing game where the correct sequence of colours is drawn out gradually. A Mastermind career is what most of us have in life. We start off with some kind of summer internship that we end up hating – none of the coloured pegs are correct – and vow to steer far away from that particular company or industry. We try another job. Fail. We try a third job and even though most aspects of it suck, we are able to find some little corner of it that we might actually enjoy – boom, one peg is in the correct slot! Gradually, we fail forward in life and pick up the pieces of the broken paths to make a mosaic we call a career. We become what we did not fail at.

Yet there are other areas in life where we should not seek new inspiration. The ethical values we hold dear, for example, are there to avoid temptation and the regret it brings. Experimentation to find out if adultery or theft is your thing is a recipe for personal disaster. Life is a wide-open space of infinite possibility. You will need handrails, not as a guide but as a boundary. Most of the times say "yes!" or "screw it, let's do it!" but let your handrails be a firm "No!"

TAKEAWAY: NEVER SAY "KNOW" - DARE TO SAY "NO".

SECTION TWO:
EXPERIMENT

Experimentation is the mother of all creation. The way we learn is by trial and error be it toddlers exploring the world using the mouth or inventors crashing and burning before hitting on the right solution. Yet experimentation is a misunderstood term. It conjures up images of a nihilistic process characterized only by its randomness. In reality, successful experimentation is more like gardening, a bottom-up way to create. The gardener cannot stipulate exactly what the outcome will look like but can ensure that certain conditions are met. The opposite is the architect who has to measure things down to the smallest details and then carefully scrutinize the building process to ensure the blueprints are being followed. Architects work top-down, they start with a vision of what is to be built and then design downwards through ventilation shafts, steel structures and floorboards.

Good experimentation, like good gardening, is best summarized by the words "passionate patience." This is why successful experiments do not happen to just anyone. Penicillin might have come about by accident but it happened in the lab of Alexander Fleming, a brilliant researcher who was investigating the properties of staphylococci bacteria. The untidy office meant that some of the Petri dishes produced mould when he went away for vacation one summer in the 1920s. The rest is medical history. What we see here is not randomness but chance favouring the prepared mind. A beautiful garden doesn't grow by luck but the particularities of its final appearance, the way colours turn out and bushes position their branches, cannot be fully controlled. In life, you cannot control what people think of you and your work. "Artists do what they do. The rest is up to the zeitgeist" as playwright Arthur Miller put it. Living bottom-up relinquishes a certain amount of control whilst letting failure be an option. Hearts will be broken. Jokes fall flat. Work will be disregarded and intentions will be misunderstood. Nobody enjoys the pain of failure. What we need to arm ourselves with is a sense of "bouncebackability" where we don't become our failures and let them weigh us down in the long run.

TAKEAWAY: BE A GARDENER – PAINT WITH BROAD STROKES, LET THE DETAILS SURPRISE YOU AND WHEN YOU FAIL, FAIL FORWARD.

SECTION THREE:
X-MEN

Fratelli Guzzini is a family-owned kitchen utensils company located in Recanata, Italy, with a long, rich history of innovation. In 1938, the company began to use the scrap from cut Plexiglas sheets to produce windows for military planes. The moulding technology was similar to that used by the company to transform ox horn into cutlery, tableware and cigarette cases. After the Second World War, the next generation of heirs went a step further. Having learned the techniques of Plexiglas sheet moulding they acquired a patent to transform semi-machined Plexiglas scrap into a new raw material. This allowed them to produce sheets of whatever size and colour they needed to make tableware.

The modern design and colours of these objects soon became the foundation for the company's iconic plastic tableware.

Yet another generation of heirs came along and saw the opportunity to broaden production by adding Plexiglas lamps to the company's distinctive tableware products. They used the concave shapes of salad bowls to create a large pendant lamp that became a common kitchen feature across Europe and laid the foundation for what is today one of the most successful lightning fixture companies in the world, iGuzzini. The name even preceded Apple's appropriation of the lower case "i" by decades. What this case study illustrates is that new ideas are often existing ideas borrowed from other areas.

Nintendo's game console Wii with its ground-breaking motion-sensitive controllers used technology developed for the airbag collision systems in cars. Swedish band Roxette's 1980's megahit song *The Look* was built around a guitar riff invented by playing an Indian sitar chord on an electric guitar. Instead of merely R&D'ing - ripping off and duplicating - these creators add another R – remixing. The management consultancy McKinsey once coined the concept of a T-shaped person that has a broad general knowledge (the roof of the T) and an in-depth specialty (the vertical part of the T). Today, we should seek to be X-shaped, having an ability to take from one area and cross-fertilize with another. Maybe you should even be starfish-shaped given that more and diverse fields will create a richer flow of ideas between industries and people.

Takeaway (of the longer variety): Let the wise words of filmmaker Jim Jarmusch guide you: "Nothing is original. Steal from anywhere that resonates with inspiration or fuels your imagination. Devour old films, new films, music, books, paintings, photographs, poems, dreams, random conversations, architecture, bridges, street signs, trees, clouds, bodies of water, light and shadows. Select only things to steal from that speak directly to your soul. If you do this, your work (and theft) will be authentic. Authenticity is invaluable; originality is non-existent. And don't bother concealing your thievery – celebrate it if you feel like it". In any case, always remember what Jean-Luc Godard said:

"IT'S NOT WHERE YOU TAKE THINGS FROM - IT'S WHERE YOU TAKE THEM TO."

SECTION FOUR:
THE UNSEEN

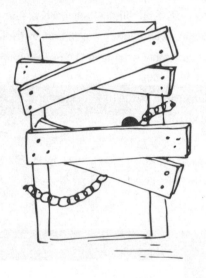

"Everything on Earth, everything ever observed with all of our instruments, all normal matter - adds up to less than 5% of the Universe." These words are from NASA and explain how we are living surrounded by a world full of secrets. Oil – the primary energy source of the planet – was for centuries hiding deep underground. New species of plants, insects and animals are continuously being discovered in the heart of the rainforest and depths of the ocean. Man-made things are also cloaked in secrecy. Xolair, an asthma drug manufactured by Novartis, revealed properties that made it a cure for a specific skin disorder called chronic idiopathic urticaria. Johan Schuster, a jobless death metal drummer from the small town Karlshamn in southern Sweden, turned out to be a magnificent pop song composer and has, under the pseudonym Shellback, enjoyed numerous number ones on the US Billboard chart.

The Spanish architect Antoni Gaudí put his finger on this when he said: "Man does not create, he discovers." Being open-minded to the secrets of people and places is the way to find hidden truths. When Silicon Valley entrepreneur Peter Thiel wants to find new ideas, he asks "what great company is nobody building?" focusing on what isn't instead of what is. The late Apple founder Steve Jobs had a similar quality. In the words of his wife, Lauren: "He saw clearly what was not there, what could be there, what had to be there. His mind was never a captive of reality."

TAKEAWAY: LOOK FOR SECRETS – IN NATURE, IN PEOPLE AND IN YOURSELF.

SECTION FIVE:
THE FLAWED RADAR

We tend to avoid truths that clash with a view of the world we hold dear. This causes hostility when we "extort confirmation of personal hypotheses that have already proved themselves to be invalid", to quote psychologist George Kelly. It explains why creators are met with such disdain by the status quo and why it is easier – more convenient – to see the world for what it is, not for what it could be. Yet only those who go too far will discover how far you can go and a society that seeks progress will always be caught in the crossfire between the old and the new. Nowhere is this more evident than inside companies.

Consider the following two categories of people, for example.

People who: | **People who:**
Look good | Are ugly
Smell good | Smell bad
Say the right things | Say strange things
Are intelligent | Are very intelligent

We tend to call people in the left column *salespeople*. They do business by making things look appealing. We tend to call people in the right column *engineers*. They are often ahead of their time where the ideas are too complex and destructively creative to translate to good business in the present. This is why sales often wins over engineering and current business revenue trumps innovation. When the right-hand column attacks the left-hand column, it is known as disruption.

Take television, for example. For a long time, TV channels invested in quality content, high-definition broadcasts and aimed to maximize the amount of viewers to lure advertisers. Then along came YouTube, full of grainy homemade video clips. A successful, national broadcaster would see no reason to worry about YouTube. At the same time came illegal bit-torrent websites where the latest movies and TV series could be downloaded for free. The national broadcaster would plead the case for the bit-torrent websites to be closed down and their hosts prosecuted. Then came online streaming services like Netflix and HBO, and all of a sudden the previously successful national broadcasters saw viewers disappear. Then came an improved YouTube, where fibre optic connections and Moore's Law – the ability of computers to become exponentially better and cheaper over time – conspired to create viewing experiences that went far beyond grainy cat videos. Today, TV broadcasters' share of viewing is shrinking and the seeds of destruction were planted right in front of them and grew silently, secretly until it was too late.

TAKEAWAY: THE BUILDING BLOCKS OF THE FUTURE ARE OBSCURED BY THE PRESENT.

SECTION SIX:
FAILURE-RECYCLING AND THE NECESSARY VIRTUE

In his book *The Happiness Hypothesis*, Jonathan Haidt argues that we might already have stumbled upon the secret to happiness but we read it long ago and were busy filling ourselves with new stimuli, more information and thus failed to stop and reflect on its significance. We assume that the future must come *from* the future and search for ideas labelled "new" when old, even ancient, ideas might be the way forward. The building material cement was used in Byzantine times but it was costly and cumbersome so it was lost for centuries until rediscovered through a new manufacturing process in the 1800s. We tend to see ideas as a "what" but they may just as well be a "when", a "who" or a "how." The song *Torn* was recorded four times, by four different artists, over four years before it became a global hit in 1997 when sung by Nathalie Imbruglia. Before the success of the iPhone, Apple released the ROKR mobile phone, a product remembered only for its dismal performance and market failure.

The virtue most often lost in the modern world is patience. Because lives are short and market cycles fast, we tend to revere such clichés as "there is no time like the present" and call for a "sense of urgency." But time does not respect human impatience, nor our vanity for that matter. Sometimes things that should happen cannot happen. Lord Byron's mathematician daughter Ada Lovelace was a computer programmer a century before there was a computer, working on Charles Babbage's Analytical Engine, a proposed mechanical general-purpose computer that was never built, due to Babbage's funding problems and fall-outs with his chief engineer. In 1919, the world electric fair in Chicago speculated that the coming years would bring gadgets like the electric washing machine, electric trucks and electric light bulb baths. Nearly all the predictions were wrong in the short run. A century later, not only have the gadgets arrived but electricity has gone on to change the world, transforming how we live and work. Singapore's late Prime Minister Mr Lee Kuan Yew even said that Singapore exists because of one invention, the air conditioner. Where there was once a corrupt jungle outpost full of pirates and drug dealers, there now stands a haven of modernity and pinnacle of civilization, all thanks to the magic of electricity.

In other words, our predictions about electric gadgets overestimated changes in the short term but underestimated the long term. We budget too narrowly when we create, hoping that change will come quickly. If we added time, more of our endeavours would succeed. iRobot, a robotics company based in Boston, decided in the early 1990s that the market was ripe for a consumer-friendly robot. They looked at a dozen different business models and decided to focus on floor-cleaning robots. The first prototype was launched after four years. It took them another decade to launch the product in the US market and another seven years before their robotic vacuum cleaner Roomba became one of the best-selling products in the world – ever – a two-decade-long route to success. The Nespresso coffee machine took nearly four decades from patent to mass-market success. We should, in fact, refer to entrepreneurship as "entrepreneurshit" since it entails years of fruitless meetings, failures and abuse. It takes years to become an overnight success, as someone wisely expressed.

TAKEAWAY: FAILURE IS WHERE SUCCESS LIKES TO HIDE IN PLAIN SIGHT.

SECTION SEVEN:
SMALL > BIG

When people tell stories about The Future, the narratives tend to be grandiose visions. Artificial Intelligence making humans superfluous. Climate change making Earth inhabitable. A belligerent clash of civilizations. The fall of the West, the rise of the rest. Big stories that claim to forecast tomorrow's world. Yet the future is not a story and there is no recipe to create it. A recipe is, by definition, a means of repeating the past whether it is baking a cupcake or building a company. There is no recipe but there are ingredients, clues that we can use to craft a future for ourselves, as opposed to the grandiose vision called Future described above. Let these ingredients be small, even trivial. Great things can be accomplished by small ideas.

Take the night-time drive made by Jim McLamore in the 1950s in Florida. He had just tasted a heavenly hamburger near Jacksonville in a run-down shack with doors falling off the hinges. The place was a dump, but the burger was so good he decided he wanted to recreate it in his own restaurant in Miami. To help him along the way, he mixed a homebrew of lemonade and bourbon and was now slowly getting drunk while driving back south. Somehow, McLamore managed to make it home safely and launched his recreated burger a few months later under the name "Whopper", which transformed his restaurant Instaburger King into a global franchise (dropping the "Insta.") This anecdote is not a recipe. If we drink-drive tonight, chances are we will be arrested, crash or, at least, wake up with a hangover. The story of Jim McLamore is an illustration of how a personal moment, a one-of-a-kind experience, was transformed into something big. Small ideas are more sustainable than big ideas because a small idea fails on a small scale whereas a big failure risks blowing up the planet. Experimentation is not about doing random things with no sense of direction while risking life and limb; it is a passionate pursuit of secrets, failure-recycling and staying patient throughout, not judging our failures too harshly or celebrating successes too enthusiastically.

TAKEAWAY: FUTURE IS A PERSONAL SPACE, NOT A PLACE ON THE TIMELINE.

PART SEVEN

FAILED
FUTURE
THINKING

SECTION ONE:
THE CRACKED CRYSTAL BALL

There is an entire industry built on the back of our failed future thinking. It is called self-storage. Scattered around our industrial estates and suburban wastelands are vast facilities housing never-used gym equipment, garments worn only once and furniture in transit waiting for divorce proceedings to be finalized. Our lives are a series of hypotheses that we seek to support, not reject. Denial is an integral part of putting up with a bad marriage or abusive boss. Suddenly our vision of what the future holds disintegrates. It is painful, even shameful. We tear up the old life up by its roots, put all its monuments and props in a self-storage warehouse and start looking for a new hypothesis while healing the scars of a future lost.

Life is all about losing yourself and finding yourself again. Yet the normalcy of turbulence in life takes us by surprise every single time. Just as remarrying is famously a triumph of hope-over-experience, we can spend our entire lives mis-predicting things and still hope we get it right the next time (to paraphrase the words of author Nassim Taleb). The irony is that 21st century living is significantly more reliant on predicting tomorrow correctly. A few centuries ago, our families, social class and geography decided for us who we should marry, where we would live and the work we should do. Today, teenagers are expected to narrow down what they want to be in life when choosing a college degree and 20-somethings have an entire world of travel destinations, internships, drugs and sexualities to explore, while 30-somethings are continuously asked about when and who they will marry and whether they want children.

In your 40s, pension fund salesmen show vast charts of where and how you should invest, while in your 50s, you may decide to re-marry and go back to playing the singles game with a range of digital dating tools at your fingertips. Life used to be cruel, brutish and short, in the words of Thomas Malthus. 21st century life is demanding in a different way. It overloads us with information then leaves us to our own devices regarding what decisions to make. No wonder we often fail. If only our brains had mutated to feature a crystal ball into which we could gaze and asses what action to take today. Alas, the gift of prophecy exists only in fairy tales and astrology, but the good news is that there are a few common mis-predictions we succumb to when thinking about the future.

TAKEAWAY: OUR ABILITY TO THINK AHEAD IS BROKEN AND WILL LEAD US ASTRAY EVERY NOW AND THEN.

SECTION TWO:
THE UNCHANGING SELF

There is approximately an hour to go before your lunch appointment is due to take place. You planned it months ago when running into a friend you had not seen since university and although you were too busy to have a coffee with her at the time, you assumed that a couple of months down the road things would have calmed down sufficiently for you to take time out of your busy schedule to reconnect with an old acquaintance. Today, however, you are as swamped as ever and not at all excited about the lunch date. In fact, you wish she would call a rain check so you could postpone the lunch yet again. She is a bit of a bore, truth to be told, and you only agreed to meet up with her to be nice. This is how all of us tend to deal with unpleasant things –

from minor surgical procedures to family social gatherings – postponing them and hoping they will magically disappear somewhere ahead of us.

People often joke that the best place to hide a dead body is on page two of Google's search results. An even better place to hide things we want to get rid of is in the future. The reason for this is that we assume things will be sufficiently different tomorrow transforming what is unpleasant today into a source of joy. The mistake we make is not necessarily that we overestimate change in general – gadgets and hemlines will indeed be different a couple of years from now – but that we take ourselves out of the equation. This is common when planning for a summer vacation and envisioning ourselves becoming a good spouse, a good parent, making time for physical workouts and starting work on reducing the "to read" pile of books that have been gathering dust on the bedside table. Summer arrives; we go away, only to find ourselves the same, warts and all. When it comes to things we find unpleasant and tend to postpone – reading a 700-page book or sweating at the gym, we should assume that we will find them equally unpleasant tomorrow so decide either to deal with them now or admit we will never do so.

When it comes to pleasant things, the exact opposite is true. Instead of thinking that things will be different, we assume we will enjoy doing the exact same thing this time next year. When we revisit our favourite restaurant or see our favourite movie yet again, we feel that something has changed but cannot quite put our finger on it. The restaurant has the same friendly staff but something is just lacking this time. The movie that once moved you to tears now seems trite and overlong. This is not because the restaurant or movie has changed but because you have.

More specifically, what it takes to stir your emotions has changed. Our emotions are like muscles and our experiences are like weightlifting sessions. What was once heavy, emotionally charged and moving now breezes by and underwhelms you. Our minds, once expanded by new experiences, never regain their original dimensions.

TAKEAWAY: WHAT FEELS BAD TODAY WILL FEEL BAD OR WORSE TOMORROW. WHAT FEELS GOOD TODAY WILL FEEL DIFFERENT TOMORROW.

SECTION THREE:
A SMALLER NEEDLE
IN A LARGER HAYSTACK

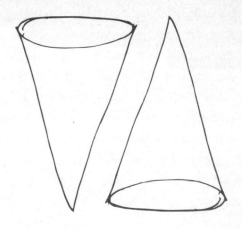

There is a paradox at the heart of future thinking. The Future – the oceans of time ahead of the planet – is without boundaries and of infinite possibility. The personal future on the other hand is shrinking with time slowly-but-surely slipping away like sand in an hourglass. The paradox manifests itself as a conflict between what we perceive as possible in our lifetime and in the very distant future. A young person will be more open-minded about possibilities because many of the things he or she dreams about actually might happen in his or her lifetime. The 68-year-old might angrily retort that certain things are impossible, even dangerous, and feel envious that he or she will not get to see the many marvels that the future will bring. This is why the future becomes more specific the older we get, like a lens zooming in rather than a cone opening up.

It is important to note that this is primarily a construct in our minds. You could live every day with a new experience to expand your horizons continuously, but most of us settle in our ways, travel less and then to the same places every year. We reside in a state of wisdom rather than curiosity. It is almost as if the brain operated with a kind of computer programme where the early years are characterized by exploration, the middle years by exploitation and the final years by memories. Yet the future is not finite. There is no chequered flag planted in the ground somewhere ahead of us in time announcing our arrival to the mythical place we have spent so much time thinking about. We die, but life, in a broader sense, continues. Is there a way to hack the programme of the brain? The renowned author Marcel Proust once said that to avoid seeing someone, you should marry them, since we tend not to notice the things we are around on a daily basis – call it invisibility by familiarization. "Extreme" sports become just another sport. "Big" Data becomes mere data. Life takes things from the shock of the new and transforms them into a sigh of the familiar. The botanist Carl Linnaeus urged us to reverse this process when he wrote: "*Omni mirari etiam tritissia* – marvel over everything, especially the most ordinary things."

TAKEAWAY: WE NEVER HAVE JUST ONE CHOICE OF WHAT TO BE OR DO IN LIFE, REGARDLESS OF AGE.

SECTION FOUR:
ATTACK OF THE UNEXPECTED

No matter how much detail we put into our maps of tomorrow, the unexpected has a nasty habit of taking us by surprise. The word itself – unexpected – is used to describe sudden, previously unimaginable phenomena in our world – from terrorist strikes and other disasters to lottery wins and blind dates. In fact, what the word "unexpected" really describes is the boundaries of our imagination. Unexpected, like abnormal or unhealthy, is a negating word where its acronym, "expected", is seen as the norm. This corresponds to the scientific experiment we call life wherein we post hypotheses about what makes us happy or not thereby outlining a territory marked by a big "To Be Expected" sign.

This territory, however, looks completely different depending on where and when you are. The death of a child is fortunately rare – unexpected – in Sweden or Switzerland but not in Swaziland. Envisioning hijacked planes flying into buildings was inconceivable on 10 September 2001 but has been a plausible scenario ever since. Angry Birds was a slur on feminists before 2010 and is now a game and Finland's most famous export. "Unexpected" is what we exclaim when something crosses the border between the land of the unimaginable, call it Unimagina, into the land of the familiar, call it Familiria. We can outline six ways in which we exile things to Unimagina, even when they should have been citizens of Familiria:

Things that happened long ago: "Unexpected" does not imply "unhappened". We have 10,000-year storms and financial crises long forgotten. This is why ancient wisdom matters in a modern world.

Things that are uncomfortable to think about: Doom-mongers make us unhappy. The fact that we will all die some day is best left ignored so that we can get busy living while there is time.

Things that are not visual: How we feel, what we taste and what we hear tend to be important ingredients in the things we enjoy or dislike but when we think about the future, we stay firmly within the visual realm – we even call it en*visioning*. The things that cannot be visualized tend to be a lot harder to imagine.

One-man shows: These are the kind of stories that tabloids love; a madman massacring innocent civilians – visual, personal and completely impossible to predict. The human mind is mysterious, full of thoughts so secret the might only exists subconsciously. "Out of the crooked timber of humanity, no straight thing was ever made," as philosopher Immanuel Kant put it.

Complexity: These are the kind of stories that tabloids hate. First, because they are not stories at all. They are just a confluence of various forces that conspire to create something we have never experienced before. The vast range of books trying and failing to explain 2008's financial crisis is a good illustration of complexity's contest of wits.

We want surprises: The best things in life are unexpected, which is why we have surprise parties and disguise presents using elaborate, decorative paper. Unexpected events create the Hollywood drama opera composers and theatre directors thrive on and we love to consume. Fortunes are made by chance encounters, happy accidents and serendipitous events. If we were given a fortune cookie with the exact time and place of our demise, most of us would throw it away. Surprises – of all kinds – make life worth living.

TAKEAWAY: THE UNEXPECTED WILL FOREVER CAST ITS SHADOW ON OUR FUTURES.

CONCLUSION:
THE FUTURE ILLUSION

THE 39 TAKEAWAYS OF THIS BOOK ARE AS FOLLOWS:

1. Go on, be a deviant!
2. Don't see your life as a story – see it as a plotless spectacle!
3. Be a pessimist if you want to seem smart, an optimist if you want to seem stupid or a possibilist if you want to be right... in the long run.
4. Savour the moment when others call you an idiot – it might mean you are on the right path.
5. Ignore the predictions of those who don't move your mind in an interesting, unexpected direction and of those who haven't had the confidence to put a lot at stake in their decisions.
6. When stuck in the midst of a dilemma, always add a third choice even, or especially, if it scares you.
7. The future hides in nothingness.
8. The future is richer, more diverse and more fragmented than today.
9. The future takes and the future gives. Ensure that your thinking is equally multi-dimensional.
10. Think magic – beyond gadgets.
11. Don't settle for a "good" idea when the weird, wacky and wild ideas are needed to change the world.
12. When used well, the cone of uncertainty has the same properties as a mind-altering drug.

13. There are four shades of "then" – from the quick, fashion changes on the street to the century-long changes we can only see from space.
14. Want to make a fast buck? Think microtrends. Want to change the world? Think gigatrends.
15. The future will require us to sacrifice the now on the altar of the then.
16. Feel good or think right?
17. The future is not smooth but jagged, discontinuous and full of "oohs", "ahhs" and "ha-has".
18. Seek to have the mind of a child. Embrace the thrill of the new.
19. Don't start with a white sheet of paper to get ideas, start with a plane ticket or a search engine to rip-off and duplicate.
20. We are capable of uniqueness but succumb to sameness over time.
21. Comparison is the thief of all joy. Competition is the thief of big ideas.
22. The future begins when we let go of the past.
23. The gravitational pull of the past means we pay an invisible price when we cling to it.
24. Dare to live vertically. You will not regret it.
25. Creation, like gold, is rare, difficult to obtain and very valuable.
26. You may be on the wrong mountain.
27. Being wrong is a portal to the future.
28. Creation is a solo endeavour.
29. Never say "know" – dare to say "no".
30. Be a gardener – paint with broad strokes, let the details surprise you and when you fail, fail forward.

31. "It's not where you take things from - it's where you take them to."
32. Look for secrets – in nature, in people and in yourself.
33. The building blocks of the future are obscured by the present.
34. Failure is where success likes to hide in plain sight.
35. Future is a personal space, not a place on the timeline.
36. Our ability to think ahead is broken and will lead us astray every now and then.
37. What feels bad today will feel bad or worse tomorrow. What feels good today will feel different tomorrow.
38. We never have just one choice of what to be or do in life, regardless of age.
39. The unexpected will forever cast its shadow on our futures.

The list leads us to a 40th takeaway, which will turn everything on its head: The future is not a noun, it is a verb – <u>to</u> future. The idea of the future as a noun – a place or a thing – misleads us into thinking we could see it if we only climbed high enough or had access to some as yet uninvented technology. Books treating the future as a fixed destination become works of science fiction demarked only by their gradual fade into irrelevance. What this book has been conveying is that we need "to future" more often. Futuring entails thinking about the world in new ways, creating instead of competing, taking a contrarian view and daring to venture where others do not.

When we use the phrase future-proofing, we do not mean that we should accurately predict next week's lottery numbers or anticipate exactly what career has the highest future payoff. Future-proofing is about having a wide-open mind and making "intellectual acupuncture" part of your daily ritual. You know you have futured when you laugh with amusement, frown in bewilderment or feel your heart race from the adrenaline-jolt of provocation. As British biologist JBS. Haldane put it: "The universe is not only stranger than we imagine, it is stranger than we can imagine."

We have words for people who dare to future and enrich the world with their creations. We call them dangerous.
We call them idiots.
Or we simply say they are aloof and unrealistic.
Later, when they succeed, we call them heroes.

ABOUT THE AUTHOR

MAGNUS LINDKVIST is a trendspotter and futurologist. He calls his work "intellectual acupuncture" aiming to change how we think about the future by provoking us with ideas, enabling new questions and challenging our world view. He lives in Stockholm, Sweden together with his wife Vesna and two children.

CONTACT THE AUTHOR FOR ADVICE, TRAINING, OR SPEAKING OPPORTUNITIES:
www.magnuslindkvist.com

ALSO BY THE AUTHOR:
Everything We Know Is Wrong, 2009
The Attack of The Unexpected, 2010
When The Future Begins, 2013
The Minifesto, 2016